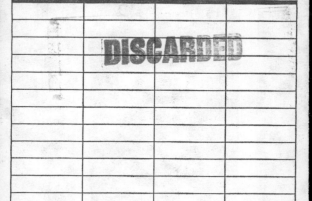

# THE NEW BOOK OF

# SPACE

## Robin Scagell

### COPPER BEECH BOOKS
### BROOKFIELD, CONNECTICUT

# Contents

© Aladdin Books Ltd 1997
© U.S. text 1997
*Designed and
produced by*
Aladdin Books Ltd
28 Percy Street
London W1P 0LD

*First published in the
United States in 1997 by*
Copper Beech Books,
an imprint of
The Millbrook Press
2 Old New Milford Road
Brookfied, CT 06804

Printed in Belgium
All rights reserved

*Editor*
Jon Richards
*Design*
David West
Children's Book Design
*Designer*
Flick Killerby
*Illustrators*
Richard Rockwood
Ian Thompson
*Picture Research*
Brooks Krikler Research

Library of Congress Cataloging-in-Publication Data
Scagell, Robin. The new book of space / Robin Scagell ;
illustrated by Ian Thompson, Richard Rockwood.
p. cm.
Includes bibliographical references and index.
Summary: Computer-generated artwork portrays developments in space
exploration and astronomy
ISBN 0-7613-0619-6 (lib. bdg.). — ISBN 0-7613-0634-X (pbk.)
1. Astronomy—Juvenile literature. 2. Astronomy in art—Juvenile literature
3. Computer animation—Juvenile literature.
[1. Astronomy. 2. Astronomy in art. 3. Computer animation.]
I. Thompson, Ian 1964- ill. II. Rockwood, Richard, ill. III. Title.
QB46.S257 1997                                    97-11143
520—dc21                                            CIP AC
5 4 3 2 1

## INTRODUCTION

The universe is so large that astronomers (people who study the stars) still do not know how big it is! However, with the technological advances of recent years, we have been learning a lot more about our place in the cosmos.

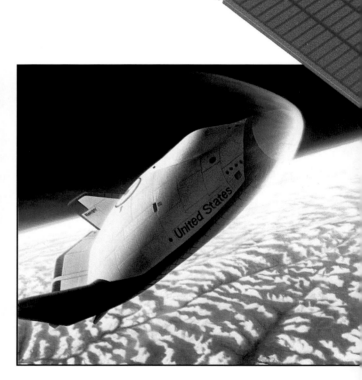

In the last fifty years, humans have been able to leave the confines of our planet. No longer content with just looking at the universe through a telescope, we can now explore the frozen expanse of space. Today, high-tech satellites hang in orbit around our planet, gazing into the depths of space, peeling away many of the mysteries of the cosmos. They have revealed some amazing phenomena that only a short time ago many astronomers would have thought impossible. These include new planets and black holes.

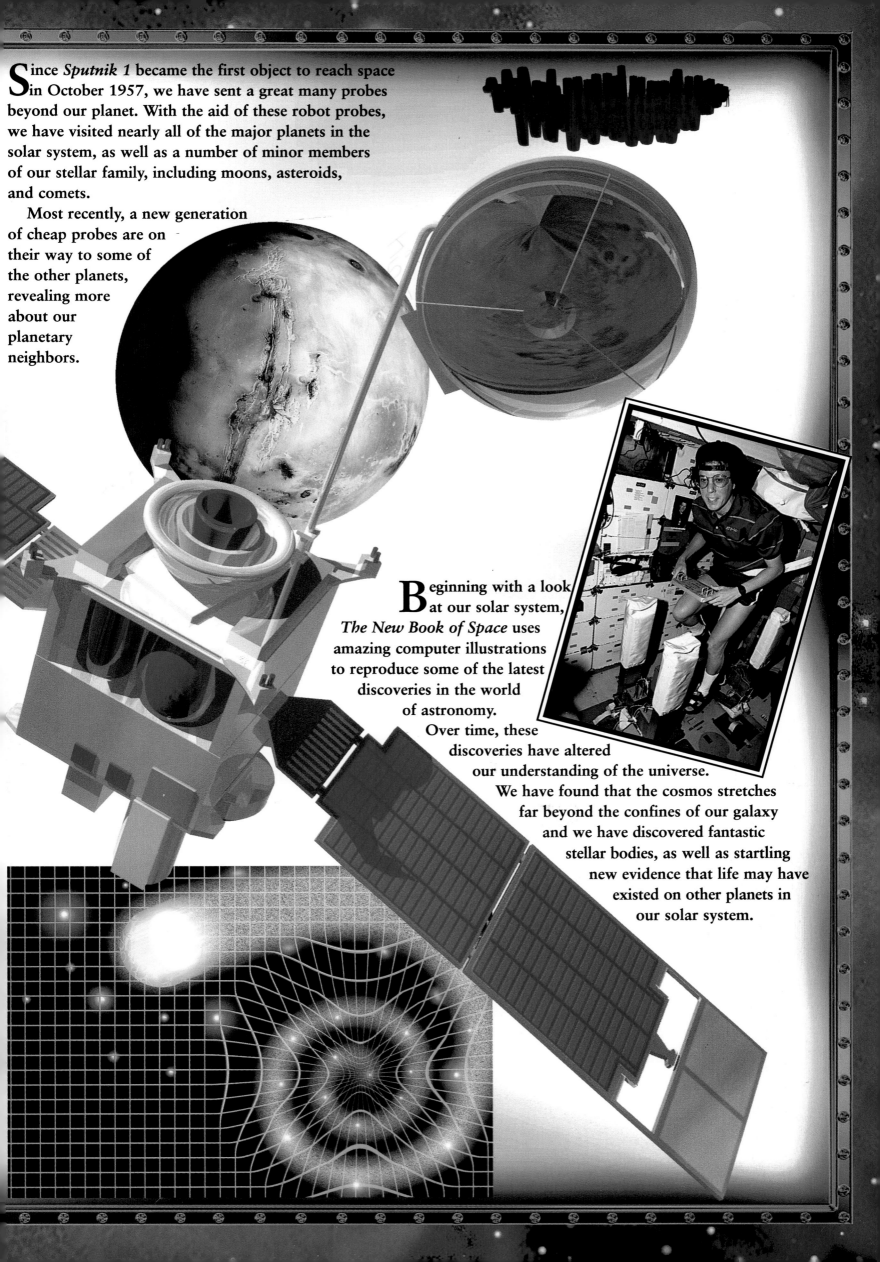

Since *Sputnik 1* became the first object to reach space in October 1957, we have sent a great many probes beyond our planet. With the aid of these robot probes, we have visited nearly all of the major planets in the solar system, as well as a number of minor members of our stellar family, including moons, asteroids, and comets.

Most recently, a new generation of cheap probes are on their way to some of the other planets, revealing more about our planetary neighbors.

Beginning with a look at our solar system, *The New Book of Space* uses amazing computer illustrations to reproduce some of the latest discoveries in the world of astronomy. Over time, these discoveries have altered our understanding of the universe. We have found that the cosmos stretches far beyond the confines of our galaxy and we have discovered fantastic stellar bodies, as well as startling new evidence that life may have existed on other planets in our solar system.

# Into SPACE

We live on a small, rocky planet, the Earth, orbiting an ordinary star, the Sun. Our nearest neighbors, the inner planets, include Mercury, Venus, and Mars. The other planets, Jupiter, Saturn, Uranus, Neptune, and Pluto, lie outside the asteroid belt, an orbiting band of small rocky chunks.

The solar system measures 7 billion miles (12 billion km) across – it takes light from the Sun over five-and-a-half hours to travel to Pluto! And yet, this family of planets forms only a tiny part of The Milky Way (*see* pages 16-17).

This chapter will show our attempts to explore the planets, including the very latest missions that are underway, or will soon be underway, to some of the planets orbiting our Sun. It will reveal many new discoveries made about our solar system, including the possibility of life on other planets.

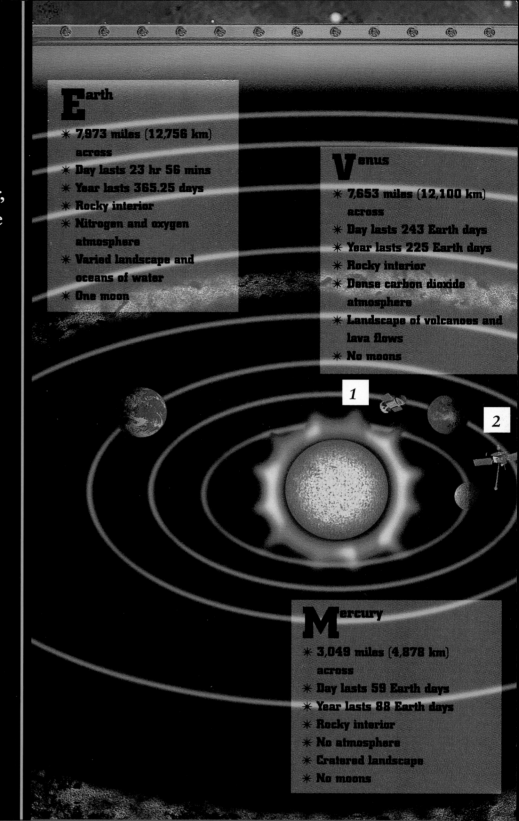

**Earth**
* 7,973 miles (12,756 km) across
* Day lasts 23 hr 56 mins
* Year lasts 365.25 days
* Rocky interior
* Nitrogen and oxygen atmosphere
* Varied landscape and oceans of water
* One moon

**Venus**
* 7,653 miles (12,100 km) across
* Day lasts 243 Earth days
* Year lasts 225 Earth days
* Rocky interior
* Dense carbon dioxide atmosphere
* Landscape of volcanoes and lava flows
* No moons

**Mercury**
* 3,049 miles (4,878 km) across
* Day lasts 59 Earth days
* Year lasts 88 Earth days
* Rocky interior
* No atmosphere
* Cratered landscape
* No moons

## REACHING SPACE

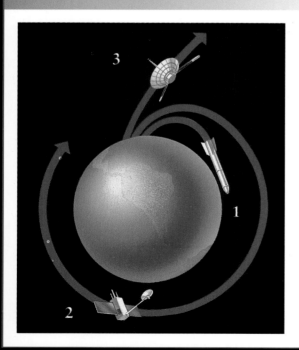

How do probes get into space? Some rockets, such as those designed to reach only the upper atmosphere (1 – *left*), do not travel fast enough to make it into space.

To get beyond the atmosphere, a rocket has to travel fast enough to overcome the pull of the Earth's gravity. A rocket that reaches a speed of 17,800 mph (28,500 km/h) is traveling so fast that the ground falls away as quickly as gravity drags the rocket down. As a result, it flies in a circular path, orbiting around the Earth (2).

In order to escape the pull of the Earth's gravity completely (3), a rocket must go faster than 25,200 mph (40,320 km/h). Once in space, some spacecraft may use the movement of the Earth and the other planets to accelerate them to faster speeds and go farther into space. This is called the "slingshot" effect (*see* page 11).

### Uranus

* 32,500 miles (52,000 km) across
* Day lasts about 17 hr
* Year lasts 84 Earth years
* Water and rock interior
* Hydrogen, helium, and methane atmosphere
* Featureless, blue-green disk
* 15 known moons

### Pluto

* 1,528 miles (2,445 km) across
* Day lasts 6 hr 39 mins
* Year lasts 248 Earth years
* Rock and ice interior
* Thin atmosphere, probably nitrogen
* Unknown landscape
* One moon

### Mars

* 4,246 miles (6,794 km) across
* Day lasts 24 hr 37 mins
* Year lasts 1.88 Earth years
* Rocky interior
* Thin carbon dioxide atmosphere
* Landscape of deserts and craters
* Two tiny moons

### Neptune

* 48,400 km (30,250 miles) across
* Day lasts about 16 hr
* Year lasts 165 Earth years
* Water and rock interior
* Hydrogen, helium, and methane atmosphere
* 8 known moons

### Saturn

* 75,000 miles (120,000 km) across
* Day lasts 10 hr 39 mins
* Year lasts 29.5 Earth years
* Gas interior
* Hydrogen and helium atmosphere
* Pale yellow belts
* At least 18 moons

### Jupiter

* 89,250 miles (142,800 km) across
* Day lasts 9 hr 55 mins
* Year lasts 11.9 Earth years
* Gas interior
* Hydrogen and helium atmosphere
* Colored bands and belts
* 16 known moons

## THE OUTER LIMITS

Several probes have been sent to the inner planets, including the *Venera* probes to Venus (1 – *see main picture*), the *Mariner* probes to Mercury (2), and *Viking* probes to Mars (3). Probes to the outer planets include *Pioneer 10* and *Pioneer 11* (4), launched in 1972 and 1973, which visited Jupiter and Saturn. *Voyager 1* and *Voyager 2* (5), launched in 1977, visited Jupiter, Saturn, Uranus, and Neptune. Some of these these probes are now on the very edge of the solar system and may continue sending back data until about 2020.

# To the MOON

Once again, our nearest neighbor, the Moon, is the target of space exploration. In the past, attention focused on getting the first humans to use its surface. Today, the aim is to use the Moon as a good source of valuable minerals.

Several unmanned probes, including *Lunar Prospector* from the United States and *Lunar-A* from Japan, are soon to start studying the Moon. Their role is to discover more about what lies on and beneath its surface.

The Moon is 2,173 miles (3,476 km) across and orbits the Earth at a distance of 250,000 miles (400,000 km). It has no atmosphere, which means there is no wind to erode (wear down) the landscape, so its features have stayed the same for millions of years. Its huge craters – some are more than 125 miles (200 km) across – were formed by collision with huge rocks and comets. There are also massive plains, which we call "seas." These were formed by molten (liquid) rock from the Moon's interior pouring over the surface.

*The* Lunar Prospector *probe (below) was launched in September 1997. After a short time orbiting the Earth, it left for the Moon, where it arrived in lunar orbit five days after its launch.*

## LUNAR PROSPECTOR

The *Lunar Prospector* probe (*above*) is designed to find out more about what the Moon is made of. The probe carries no cameras, but has instruments that can examine the surface from an orbit 60 miles (100 km) above it. It can measure the Moon's composition and magnetism, and will search for traces of gases given off from volcanoes.

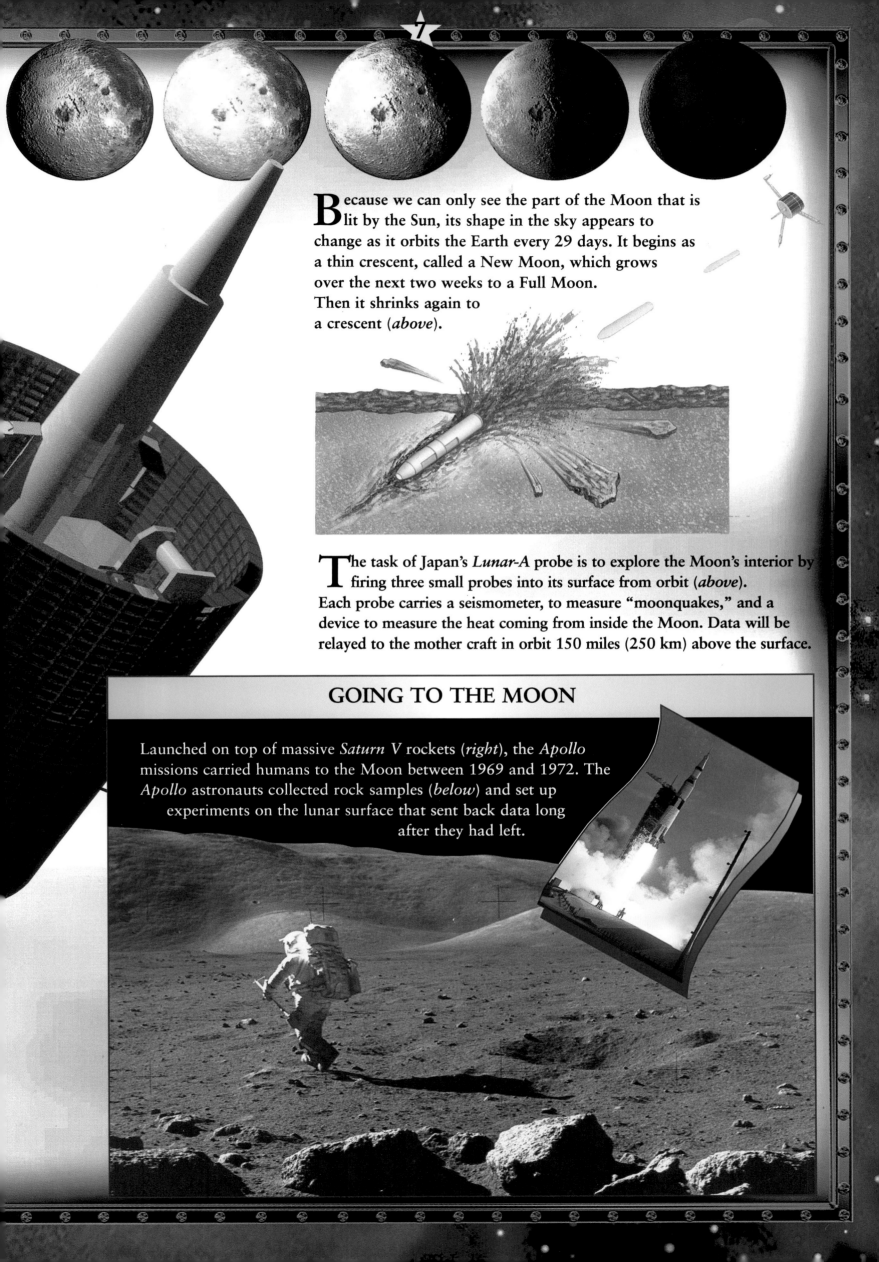

Because we can only see the part of the Moon that is lit by the Sun, its shape in the sky appears to change as it orbits the Earth every 29 days. It begins as a thin crescent, called a New Moon, which grows over the next two weeks to a Full Moon. Then it shrinks again to a crescent (*above*).

The task of Japan's *Lunar-A* probe is to explore the Moon's interior by firing three small probes into its surface from orbit (*above*). Each probe carries a seismometer, to measure "moonquakes," and a device to measure the heat coming from inside the Moon. Data will be relayed to the mother craft in orbit 150 miles (250 km) above the surface.

## GOING TO THE MOON

Launched on top of massive *Saturn V* rockets (*right*), the *Apollo* missions carried humans to the Moon between 1969 and 1972. The *Apollo* astronauts collected rock samples (*below*) and set up experiments on the lunar surface that sent back data long after they had left.

# T he Red PLANET

Mars has thrown up some amazing developments in recent times. Probes have landed on its surface for nearly 20 years – a total of ten missions are planned by 2005. Evidence has also been discovered indicating the possibility that life may have existed on the Red Planet in the past.

Although Mars might look a little like a desert, conditions there are much harsher. As the next planet out from the Earth, Mars is much colder than it. It is also smaller, and has much less atmosphere. The air is far too thin to breathe, and it is mostly carbon dioxide. Despite a few thin clouds in the sky, the surface is almost completely dry. But Mars was not always like this. In the past it was warmer, with more atmosphere, and great floods of water poured through the now dried-up valleys.

## LIFE ON MARS

In 1996, scientists reported that a meteorite found in Antarctica had the same composition as Martian rocks. It probably fell to Earth after Mars was hit by a comet. Inside the rock are strange features (*right*) that may be fossils of simple bacteria.

A huge gash in Mars' surface (*below*), called Valles Marineris, is a system of cracks and canyons. Some of these show signs that water used to flow on Mars. Elsewhere on the planet there are deserts of sand dunes. These deserts are bigger than Earth's Saharan and Arabian deserts put together.

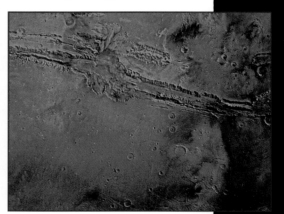

*Mars* Pathfinder *landed in a former floodplain called Ares Vallis. This lies to the north of the Valles Marineris.*

## VOLCANOES

The biggest volcano in the solar system, Olympus Mons (*left*), is found on Mars. It rises 16 miles (25 km) above the surrounding plains. Millions of years ago, huge amounts of gas must have come from such volcanoes, creating a thick atmosphere around Mars. But for some reason most of this atmosphere has been lost.

Mars (*below*) *has polar caps made of solid carbon dioxide which freezes in the atmosphere. The southern cap can melt in summer, but the northern one is always there.*

The job of Mars *Global Surveyor* (*below*) is to map Mars in detail in a two-year mission. Its orbit around Mars takes it over every point on the Martian surface, repeating the same sequence every week. Its cameras are powerful enough to show objects as small as 10 ft (3 m) across – so the final maps will be more detailed than those of parts of the Earth.

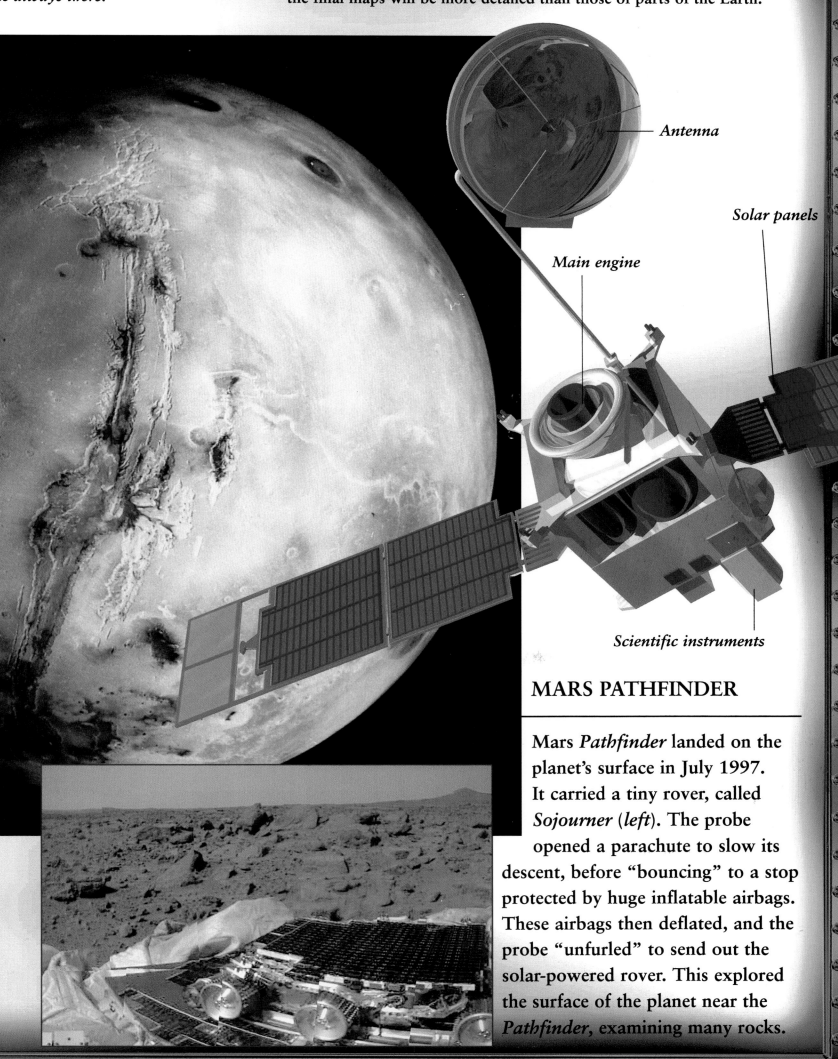

Antenna

Solar panels

Main engine

Scientific instruments

## MARS PATHFINDER

Mars *Pathfinder* landed on the planet's surface in July 1997. It carried a tiny rover, called *Sojourner* (*left*). The probe opened a parachute to slow its descent, before "bouncing" to a stop protected by huge inflatable airbags. These airbags then deflated, and the probe "unfurled" to send out the solar-powered rover. This explored the surface of the planet near the *Pathfinder*, examining many rocks.

# Jupiter & ITS MOONS

Jupiter is a planet quite unlike the Earth or Mars – it has no solid surface. This is because Jupiter is made mostly of the gases hydrogen and helium. If you tried to land on Jupiter, you would just keep falling through its clouds until the pressure and temperature became too much for your spaceship to bear. Eventually, you would be crushed and roasted. This is what happened to a small probe launched from the *Galileo* spacecraft in 1995 (*right*).

Jupiter is the biggest planet in the solar system – it is bigger than all the other planets put together. Close-up pictures show swirls and spots that change all the time. One feature, the Great Red Spot, has been there for more than 300 years. This spot is so big that the Earth could fit inside it three times. A collection of at least 16 moons orbit Jupiter. The largest of these, the Galilean moons, are Callisto, Io, Europa, and Ganymede.

*Jupiter*

Callisto (*below left*) is bigger than our Moon and has a crust of ice that has been bombarded by rocks from space. The moon is covered with chains of craters that could have been caused by pieces of comets that were broken up by Jupiter's very powerful gravity. One mystery that has been puzzling astronomers is the existence of so much dust on Callisto's icy surface.

## GALILEO SPACECRAFT

The *Galileo* spacecraft (*below*) has sent back masses of pictures and data about Jupiter. Shortly after launch, its umbrella-like antenna failed to open properly, so the craft's signals were much weaker than expected. Even so, scientists have learned a great deal from the information it has gathered. They were also able to use *Galileo* to view the collision of comet Shoemaker-Levy 9 with Jupiter (*see* page 14).

*Scientific instruments*

*Atmospheric probe*

*Fiber glass arm*

Ganymede (*right*) is the largest moon in the solar system, bigger than the planets Mercury or Pluto. Its surface is covered with grooves, which were probably caused by past stresses and strains. The *Galileo* spacecraft found that Ganymede is giving off hydrogen gas, and is the only moon to have a magnetic field.

Io (*above*) is the closest large moon to Jupiter. Its interior is churned up by Jupiter's gravity. This causes volcanoes to erupt, forming lakes of molten sulfur, giving Io its color.

*Antenna*

A probe launched by *Galileo* parachuted into Jupiter's atmosphere, taking readings as it descended. It recorded winds of 400 mph (650 km/h) and reached 100 miles (160 km) below the cloud tops. At this depth temperatures of 284°F (140°C) and high pressures destroyed it. It found less water and a clearer atmosphere than scientists expected.

## TRAJECTORY

In order to reach Jupiter with the least rocket power, *Galileo* was sent on a long orbit. After its launch in 1989 (1 – *below*) it traveled to Venus (2), then back to Earth. Each time it used the planets' own movement to boost its speed and "slingshot" it farther into the solar system. In 1991, *Galileo* went into the asteroid belt, past two asteroids, Gaspra and Ida. It sent back first close-up views of these chunks of rock (3). *Galileo* reached Jupiter in 1995 (4), releasing its probe into the planet's atmosphere. By the end of 1997, *Galileo* will have completed its mission (5).

Europa (*right*) is a ball of ice just a little smaller than our own Moon. Data sent back by *Galileo* shows that liquid water may exist below the thick, icy crust. Some scientists think that this liquid water may harbor simple forms of life, kept alive by heat and minerals welling up from Europa's interior.

# Saturn & Its Rings

When the two *Voyager* spacecraft passed Saturn (*see* page 5), they sent back some stunning pictures of the planet. To increase the information gathered by these two probes, we are sending another, called *Cassini*. This will study Saturn in more detail and drop a tiny probe onto one of its moons.

Like Jupiter, Saturn is not solid, but a great ball of hydrogen and helium gas. The spectacular rings around the planet are not as solid as they appear. Instead, they are made of billions of pieces of ice and rock (*below*). Scientists think the rings were formed by collisions between moons that got too close to Saturn.

Saturn also has at least 18 moons. No one is quite sure how many there are, because some of the smaller ones seem to come and go. They may be just clumps of ring material rather than true moons.

*Detail of Saturn's rings*

## REACHING SATURN

The probe *Cassini* is due to reach Saturn in 2004. Like the *Galileo* probe (*see* page 11), it will fly on a long orbit, swinging past Venus, the Earth, and Jupiter during a flight lasting nearly seven years. It will orbit the planet and drop a small probe, called *Huygens*, onto Titan, the largest of Saturn's moons.

## WIGGLY RINGS

At the outside edge of Saturn's main rings are a number of much narrower rings that appear to be intertwined (*below*). Scientists were puzzled by what caused these rings to do this. The answer lay in the discovery of two moons that orbit either side of the rings. The gravity of these two "shepherd" moons, called Pandora and Prometheus, bends the shape of the rings, causing them to clump together and overlap each other. These intertwined rings were first seen by the two *Voyager* spacecraft that visited Saturn between 1979 and 1980.

## TITAN'S CLOUDS

*Huygens probe*

Titan's nitrogen atmosphere contains molecules that turn the sky orange (*below*). On the surface may lie huge regions covered in a chemical called ethane. But Titan is very cold, -290°F (-180°C), so the ethane would be in a liquid form.

Saturn's rings (*left*) start about 4,350 miles (7,000 km) above the planet's clouds, and are nearly 43,750 miles (70,000 km) wide.

The rings themselves are formed of much smaller ringlets – there may be over 10,000 of these altogether.

Main parachute

Protective shield

Second parachute

## SATURN'S MOONS

Among Saturn's larger moons is Mimas, which has an enormous crater on its surface – its diameter is equivalent to a third of the entire moon. Another moon, Iapetus, is strange because one side is very bright and the other very dark, and no one knows why. Dione has cracks that make it look like an egg about to hatch.

The *Huygens* probe (*left*) will reach Titan at over 12,500 mph (20,000 km/h). The probe will be slowed by friction as it enters the atmosphere, before a number of parachutes open to give it a soft landing on the moon's surface. As it descends it will send data to the main *Cassini* probe. It can analyze the atmosphere, take measurements of the weather, and also take pictures.

*Mimas*

*Iapetus*

*Dione*

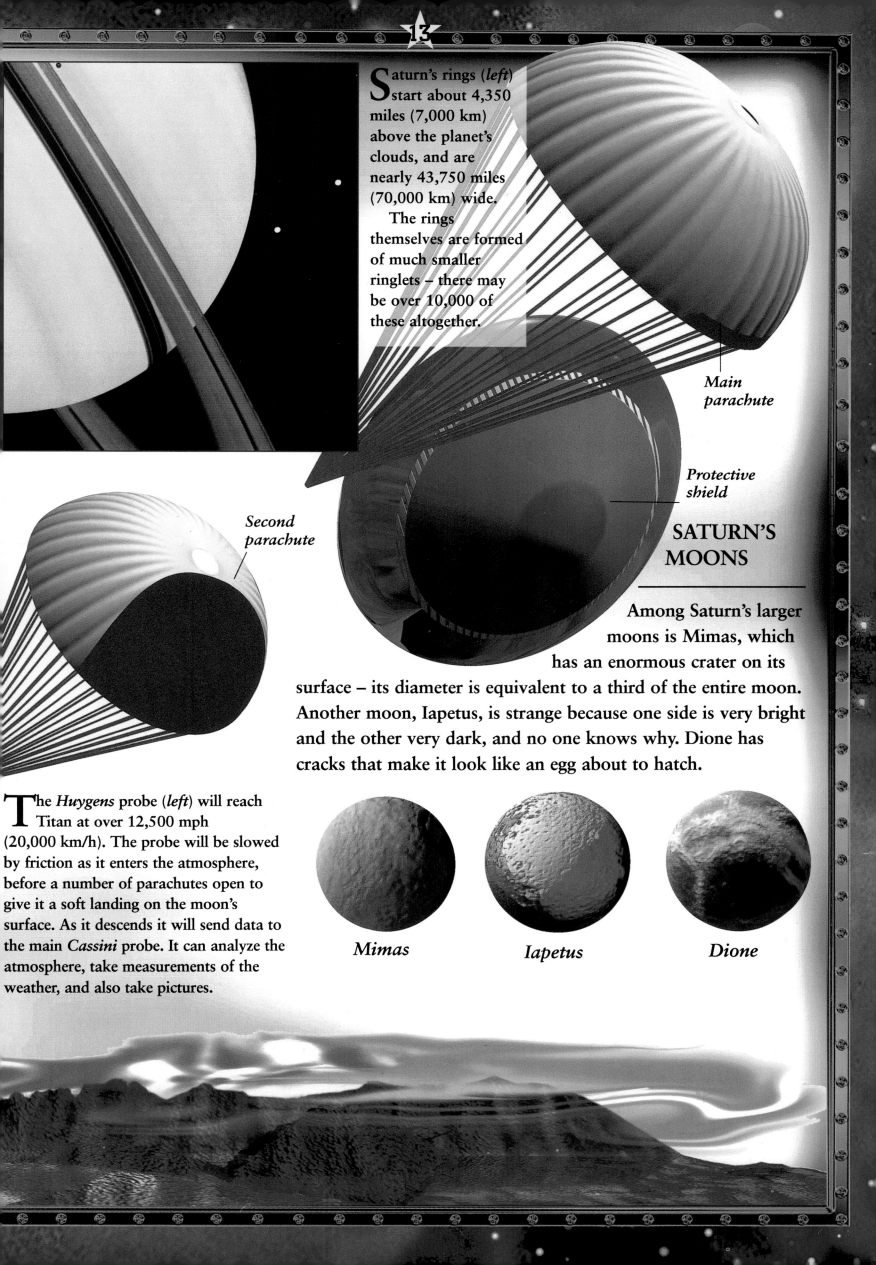

# Comets & ASTEROIDS

Comets and asteroids are among the smaller members of the solar system. Comets are basically dirty snowballs traveling through space. Occasionally, they appear in the night sky, trailing huge tails of gas and dust. The source of these huge tails is, by comparison, tiny. The nucleus of a comet may only be a few miles across, while its tails may stretch for anything up to 100 million miles (160 million km).

Asteroids are also quite small – the largest, Ceres, is only 1,600 miles (1,000 km) across, and they are made mostly of rock rather than ice. Most of them orbit between Mars and Jupiter in the asteroid belt. They are probably rocks that never collected to form a planet.

Because of their strange orbits, comets and asteroids sometimes come close and even hit one of the solar system's other planets – including the Earth. When this happens, the effects can be catastrophic!

## SHOEMAKER-LEVY 9

A dramatic event occurred in 1994 when a comet hit Jupiter. When the comet, called Shoemaker-Levy 9, was first seen, it had already broken up into 21 fragments that stretched in a line for more than 620,000 miles (one million km) (*right*). The largest pieces were probably about 2.5 miles (4 km) across. When these pieces of Shoemaker-Levy 9 crashed into Jupiter they exploded with the same force as trillions of megatons of high-explosive.

*The marks made by the impact of the comet on Jupiter (right) lasted for many months before they were erased by the planet's strong winds.*

## COMETS

A comet usually has a long, looping path and can take thousands of years to orbit the Sun. Most of its time is spent beyond the orbit of Pluto. Its tails only develop when it gets near the Sun (*left*). Some comets, such as Halley's Comet, have shorter orbits and return regularly.

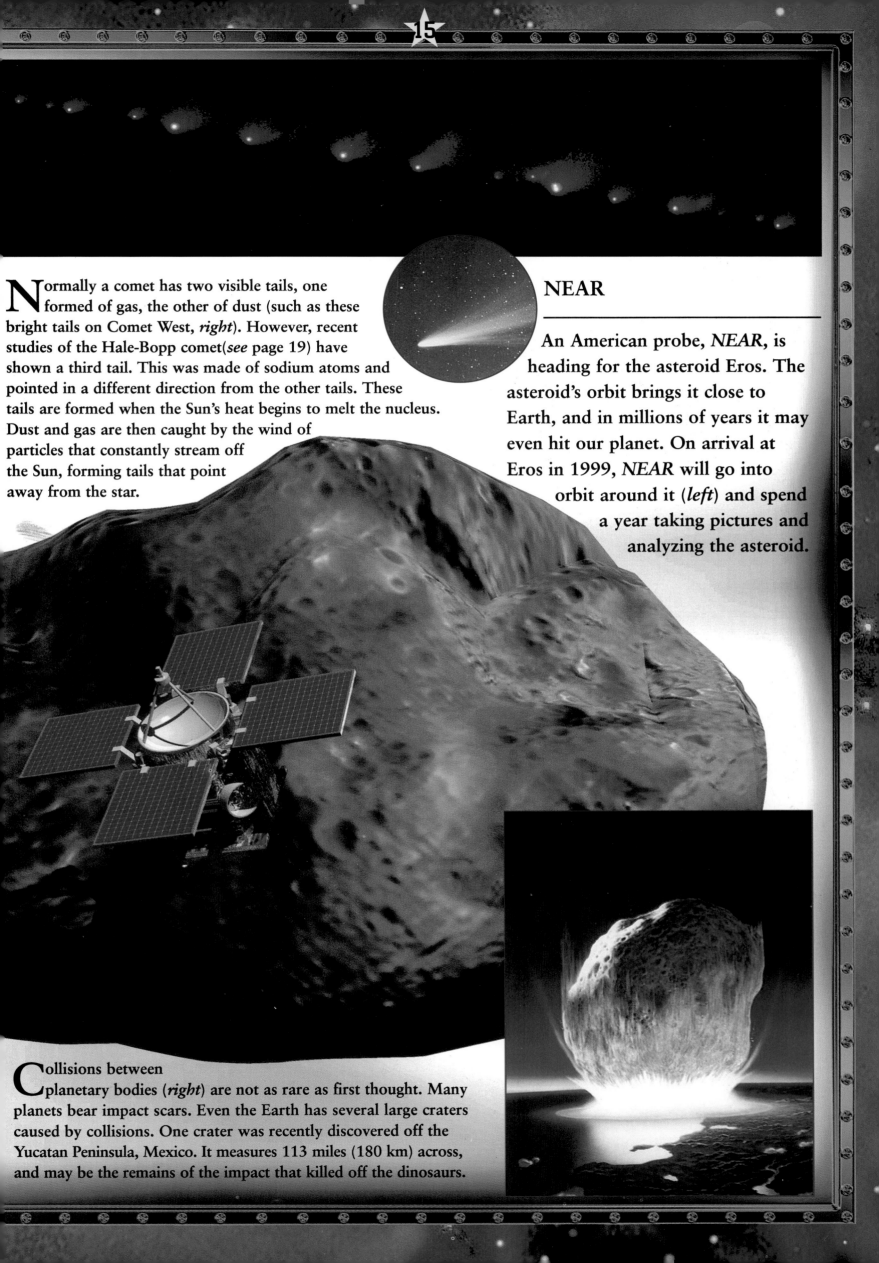

Normally a comet has two visible tails, one formed of gas, the other of dust (such as these bright tails on Comet West, *right*). However, recent studies of the Hale-Bopp comet(*see* page 19) have shown a third tail. This was made of sodium atoms and pointed in a different direction from the other tails. These tails are formed when the Sun's heat begins to melt the nucleus. Dust and gas are then caught by the wind of particles that constantly stream off the Sun, forming tails that point away from the star.

## NEAR

An American probe, *NEAR*, is heading for the asteroid Eros. The asteroid's orbit brings it close to Earth, and in millions of years it may even hit our planet. On arrival at Eros in 1999, *NEAR* will go into orbit around it (*left*) and spend a year taking pictures and analyzing the asteroid.

Collisions between planetary bodies (*right*) are not as rare as first thought. Many planets bear impact scars. Even the Earth has several large craters caused by collisions. One crater was recently discovered off the Yucatan Peninsula, Mexico. It measures 113 miles (180 km) across, and may be the remains of the impact that killed off the dinosaurs.

# The size OF SPACE

When you look at the night sky, all the stars you see are really quite close to the solar system. If the sky is clear and dark enough, you might see a faint band of light called the Milky Way. This band is a view of our own galaxy, a huge disk of stars, which we see edge-on. The Sun is just one of more than 100 billion stars that make up the Milky Way. In turn, the Milky Way is just one of billions of galaxies that lie in every direction throughout the universe.

The next pages will look at recent discoveries made by professional astronomers using the latest high-tech equipment and amateurs using more traditional methods. These discoveries are so far away that normal measurements are useless. Instead, scientists use light-years – the distance that light travels in a year. This is equivalent to 6 million million miles (10 million million km)!

*Not all galaxies have the same shape (below). Some are spiral, like our own Milky Way galaxy. Others, called elliptical galaxies, are balls of stars. But the most common type of galaxy is irregular, with no particular shape at all.*

The *Hubble Space Telescope* has photographed galaxies that are more than 11 billion light-years away (*left*). Because the light from these galaxies has taken so long to reach us, we are seeing these galaxies as they appeared 11 billion years ago. They can tell us a lot about how the universe formed and, perhaps, how it will die.

*Galaxies seen in space*

# THE MILKY WAY

Our own Milky Way Galaxy is a flat disk of stars, about 120,000 light-years across, with a central bulge. The stars in the disk are arranged in a spiral structure. The huge spiral arms contain the clouds of dust and gas where new stars are born (*right*).

*Our Sun is found some 30,000 light-years from the middle of the Milky Way, in an area called the Orion Arm (above). Scientists have recently discovered that a huge black hole may lie at the center of the galaxy.*

Scientists have known for many years that the universe is expanding – information from distant galaxies has shown that they are flying apart from each other. Because of this, they believe that the universe was created by a huge explosion, the Big Bang. From this all the stars, planets, and galaxies were formed. The universe may go on expanding forever, but some people believe this expansion will eventually slow down. The universe may then start to contract, ending with the opposite of the Big Bang – the Big Crunch.

The Milky Way is just one of a clump of neighboring galaxies, called the Local Group. In turn, the Local Group forms part of a much bigger collection of galaxies called a cluster, which is also part of a supercluster. These huge structures can measure 100 million light-years across! Altogether, scientists estimate that the universe may contain more than one hundred billion galaxies.

# Amateur ASTRONOMERS

Spending many hours sitting in the cold and dark, large numbers of amateur astronomers are responsible for a great many discoveries. These include finding novae or new comets, such as the Hale-Bopp comet.

Frequently, these discoveries are made by gazing at one patch of sky for long periods of time, then comparing the image in the telescope with charts of the region. Only then might they stumble across an amazing discovery.

L arge astronomical telescopes are usually called reflector-type telescopes (*below*). They use a mirror at the bottom of the tube to focus the light near the top end. A small mirror reflects the image to the side of the tube where you can make it larger by using an eyepiece. Amateur astronomers use telescopes, such as reflectors or refractors (*see below*), to see images of events such as the explosion of a star in a distant galaxy (*left*).

*North polar region*

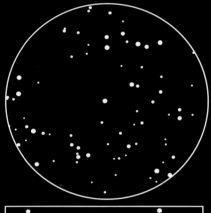

*Equatorial region*

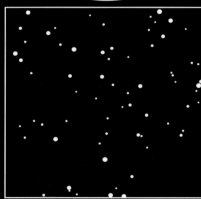
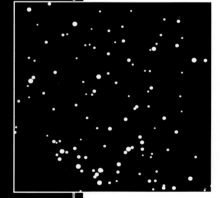

*Orion*

## STAR MAPS

Astronomers use star maps to find their way around the sky. This star map (*above*) divides the sky into the north and south polar regions (the circles above and below) and the equatorial region (the four squares running across the middle). The constellation of Orion is in the far right square. Any new objects that may appear, such as the smudge of a comet, can be compared to the star maps and catalogued.

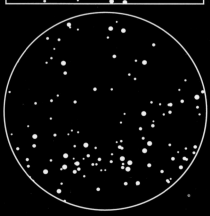

*South polar region*

As well as the discovery of a new tail (*see* page 15), scientists found out a lot from the Hale-Bopp comet (*below*). They discovered the presence of alcohol in the comet as well as traces of chemicals that form the components of living organisms. This added evidence to the theory that the "ingredients" for life on Earth actually came from passing comets, or even comets that collided with our planet.

# COMET WATCHERS

Amateur astronomers occasionally make discoveries by accident. This is how the Hale-Bopp comet (*below*) was found. Alan Hale and Thomas Bopp were each looking at the sky through their own telescopes in July 1995, when they spotted a faint object they did not recognize near a star cluster. It turned out to be a comet that had not been seen before. At its closest, the comet came within 125 million miles (200 million km) of the Earth. During its visit in 1997, the Hale-Bopp comet proved to be one of the largest comets to have orbited the Sun. Scientists have calculated that it will not return for another 4,000 years.

In contrast to a reflecting telescope, the refracting telescope (*left*) uses a lens at the top of the tube to focus the light from the object in the sky. You look through an eyepiece at the bottom end to make the image larger. Refracting telescopes are easy to use, but larger ones tend to be very expensive.

*Amateur astronomer using a refracting telescope*

# Hubble Space
## TELESCOPE

For years astronomers dreamed of putting a large telescope into space. From there it could get a clear view of the stars, undisturbed by the pollution and clouds of the Earth's atmosphere. In 1990, the dream came true when the *Hubble Space Telescope (HST)* was launched from a space shuttle. However, the project immediately ran into problems when it was realized that the main focusing mirror had been inaccurately made. In 1993, shuttle astronauts corrected the fault by adding extra lenses. Since then, the *HST* has been sending amazing pictures of all types of objects back to Earth. These include planets, nebulae (gas clouds), and quasars (*see right*). The *HST's* discoveries have improved our knowledge about the nature of the universe.

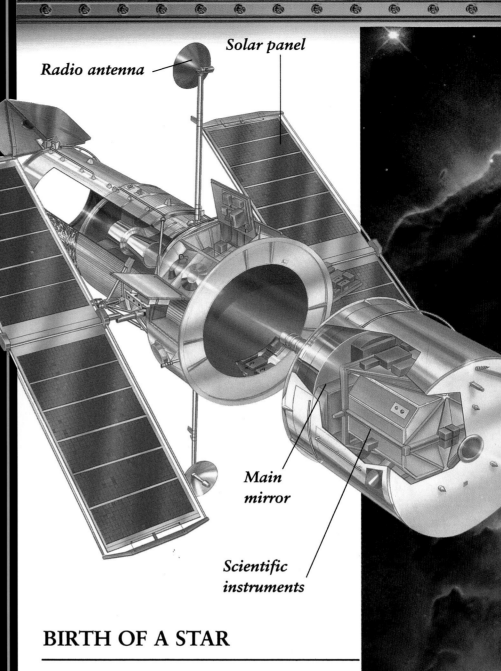

Radio antenna
Solar panel
Main mirror
Scientific instruments

*Distant galaxies seen by* Hubble

## BIRTH OF A STAR

One of *HST's* most dramatic pictures is of the Eagle Nebula (*right*), a gas cloud where stars are being born. Inside the long fingers of the cloud, gas gathers into blobs that start to contract under their own gravity. As they contract, they get hotter and hotter, until the cloud ignites to become a shining star.

A nother region where stars are being formed is the Orion Nebula (*right*). Here, the *Hubble Space Telescope* has found blobs or disks of gas called "proplyds" (short for "proto-planetary disks") surrounding very young stars (*far right*). These are thought to be the earliest stages of new planetary systems in formation. Eventually these disks will shrink down and clump together to form actual planets, like those in our own solar system.

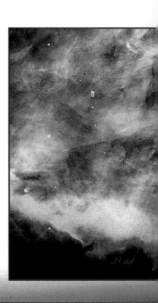

## DEATH OF A STAR

After billions of years, stars run short of the fuel that provides them with the energy they need to shine. When this fuel has run out, the star blasts its outer layers away, creating vast shells of gas around its remains. The Cat's Eye Nebula (*above*) is the result of such an event. It will last a few thousand years before fading away.

The very biggest stars explode when they run out of fuel. An exploding star is called a supernova and may leave a black hole.

The *HST* has provided the clearest proof yet that quasars (short for "quasi-stellar objects" – *left*) are really the centers of very young galaxies that are giving out huge quantities of light. The telescope's sharp pictures have shown the galaxies surrounding quasars. These are normally hidden in the glare of the galaxy's center. Astronomers believe that quasars are powered by huge black holes in the centers of newborn galaxies.

*Proplyds surrounding very young stars in the Orion Nebula.*

## SERVICING THE HUBBLE

The *Hubble Space Telescope* was designed to be serviced by astronauts from a space shuttle. Every few years they visit it to upgrade instruments or carry out repairs. The shuttle catches up with *HST*, then an astronaut uses the remote-controlled arm to bring the telescope into the cargo bay where astronauts can work on it. A recent servicing mission in 1997 (*below*) replaced many of the instruments and installed new ones, such as an infrared camera.

# Beyond the VISIBLE

There is more to the universe than what we can see. Stars and other objects are continuously sending out invisible rays. These include X rays, gamma rays, microwaves, and radio waves. Together with rays of visible light, they form what is known as the electromagnetic spectrum (*see below*).

By using special scientific instruments that can "see" the invisible parts of the spectrum, astronomers have discovered a lot more about the universe. These have included the discovery of a huge cloud of antimatter particles above our galaxy, as well as huge black holes gobbling up everything that floats around them.

Gamma rays and X rays are the most powerful rays in the electromagnetic spectrum. They are often emitted where violent astronomical events are taking place, such as around black holes. Hot stars emit large amounts of ultraviolet light, while microwaves and radio waves are a sign of clouds of cool gas.

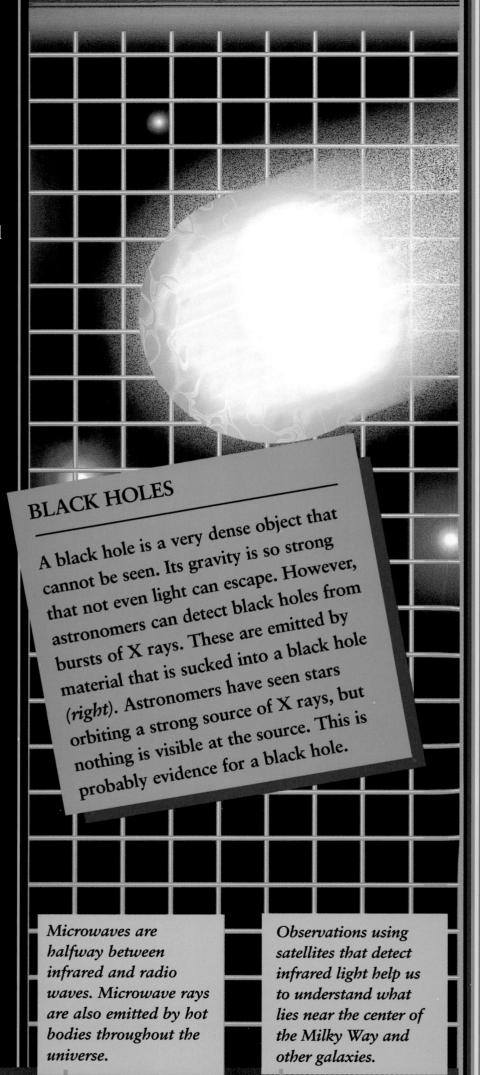

## BLACK HOLES

A black hole is a very dense object that cannot be seen. Its gravity is so strong that not even light can escape. However, astronomers can detect black holes from bursts of X rays. These are emitted by material that is sucked into a black hole (*right*). Astronomers have seen stars orbiting a strong source of X rays, but nothing is visible at the source. This is probably evidence for a black hole.

*Radio astronomers can link radio telescopes on opposite sides of the Earth to give very detailed views of the centers of other galaxies.*

*Microwaves are halfway between infrared and radio waves. Microwave rays are also emitted by hot bodies throughout the universe.*

*Observations using satellites that detect infrared light help us to understand what lies near the center of the Milky Way and other galaxies.*

## ANTIMATTER

The picture (*below*) shows the presence of a newly discovered cloud of antimatter above the center of our galaxy (the glow in the center of the picture). Scientists can "see" antimatter by detecting the gamma rays that it emits. This huge cloud of antimatter particles may have been caused by the formation of massive stars or a black hole at the center of our galaxy.

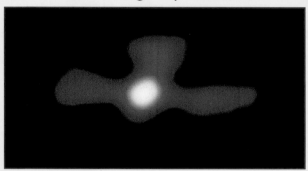

## OTHER RAYS FROM SPACE

Many other types of rays exist in the universe. Cosmic rays are made up of energetic particles that probably come from novae deep in space. Neutrinos are tiny particles emitted by the Sun. They are so small that trillions of them pass through you all the time without you noticing! However, recent studies of neutrinos indicate that there are fewer of them than scientists first calculated.

*Studying the ultraviolet light from stellar objects tells astronomers more about the reactions that occur deep within stars.*

*Some objects in space emit their own X rays, such as the hot gas surrounding black holes – collapsed stars so dense that nothing can escape their gravity.*

*Sudden bursts of gamma rays (above) have puzzled scientists. Recently, their source was traced to violent events in galaxies very far away.*

# The search FOR NEW PLANETS

The planets that orbit our own star, the Sun, are well known to us. But are there any planets orbiting other stars? Scientists believe that they should be fairly common. However, these planets would be very difficult to detect. Even the nearest star is so far away that large telescopes show it as only a point of light – any planet will be thousands of times fainter, and much harder to see.

In trying to find any new planets, scientists look for tiny variations in a star's position in space and analyze the makeup of its starlight. Recently, they have successfully detected evidence of planets around other stars and are even planning ways of photographing them.

However, the Earth is surrounded by large amounts of dust that collects around the inner planets. This dust gets in the way and makes it very difficult to see dim and distant objects. To get a clear view, we would have to send a probe into the outer solar system.

*Light split up by a compact disk*

## ABSORPTION LINES

When a star's light is split into a spectrum (*see below*) it may contain black lines, called absorption lines (*above*). These lines show where certain colors of the spectrum have been absorbed by chemicals in the star. Because certain chemicals absorb certain colors of light, scientists can tell what a star is made of. Any movement of these lines may be evidence of a planet orbiting the star.

## DISTANT WORLDS

What would it be like to stand on the planet of another star? To find another world as comfortable to live on as the Earth would be very difficult. Even in our own solar system there are no planets to match the conditions on our own planet. A planet around another star may be blasted by the radiation from its own sun, or have an atmosphere of poisonous gases (*below*).

## SPECTRUM OF COLORS

Light from a star is made up of lots of different colors that are mixed together. Scientists can split up starlight into its different colors, forming a spectrum, just like the surface of a compact disk splits up light (*left*). A star's spectrum can tell scientists a lot about it, such as what it is made of and if there are planets orbiting it (*see above*).

## DARWIN

A future project to look for planets around other stars is a space probe called *Darwin*. One design for the probe has a group of separate telescopes about 330 ft (100 m) apart linked to a central point by lasers (*below*). This probe would be placed in orbit between the planets Mars and Jupiter.

## CATCHING A SPECTRUM

To pick up small movements in the absorption lines of a star's spectrum, astronomers use Charge Coupled Devices (CCDs). Rather than using photographic film, these capture the spectrum on a silicon chip and display it on a computer screen (*left*).

A star is much bigger than a planet. Even so, the presence of a planet can still affect the star's movement. As the planet orbits the star, the planet's own force of gravity will pull the star from side to side. Astronomers see this movement as a slight wiggle in the stars motion across the sky. The amount of this wiggle in the star's path indicates the size of the planet that is orbiting around it.

# Living in SPACE

The recent events that occurred on the aging *Mir* space station have highlighted the dangers of living and working in space. Following a collision between a supply vessel and the station's solar panels, much of *Mir*'s power was lost. As a result, one of *Mir*'s modules had to be evacuated in a hurry, forcing the astronauts to leave behind valuable equipment and supplies.

Over the past thirty years, crewed space stations, such as *Mir*, have played an important role in the space program. Astronauts on board have carried out chemical and medical experiments. A range of spacecraft has been used, including, the Russian *Salyut* and American *Skylab* (*below*) stations.

Over this time we have learned a great deal about the benefits and dangers of living in space. For example, everyday things we take for granted on Earth have to be planned carefully – going to the bathroom requires special care!

Skylab *space station*

The health of astronauts in space is carefully monitored. During a long-term mission they undergo rigorous physical tests (*left*) to see how their bodies are coping with life in zero gravity. During the recent trouble with the *Mir* space station, the stress of the situation actually affected the heart rate of the crew leader, forcing a postponement of the repairs.

Training for space missions is long and tough, especially if that mission is to include space walks. Practice for recent missions, such as the servicing the *Hubble Space Telescope* and repairing the *Mir* space station, has involved many hours spent submerged in a swimming pool (*above left*). This mimics the weightless conditions found in orbit.

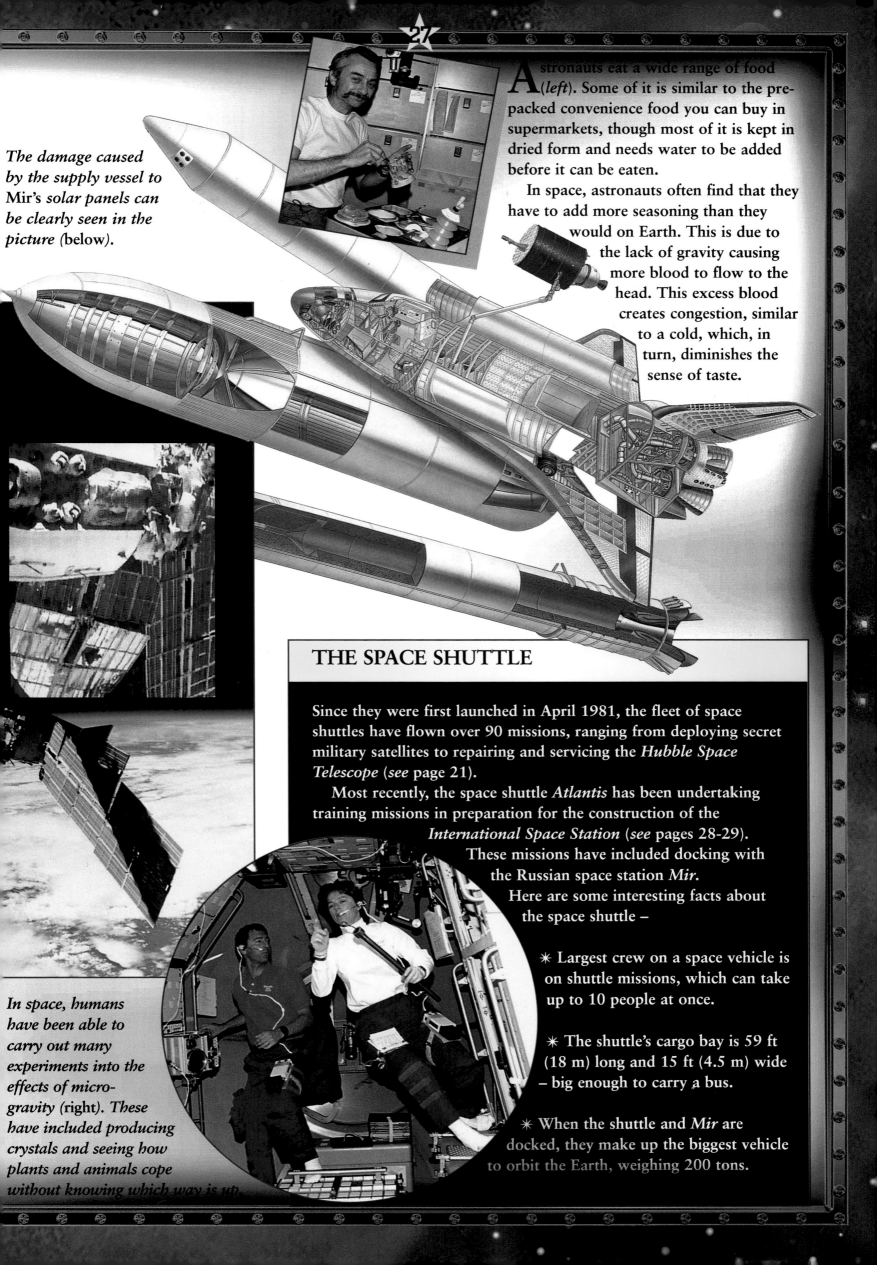

The damage caused by the supply vessel to Mir's solar panels can be clearly seen in the picture (below).

Astronauts eat a wide range of food (*left*). Some of it is similar to the pre-packed convenience food you can buy in supermarkets, though most of it is kept in dried form and needs water to be added before it can be eaten.

In space, astronauts often find that they have to add more seasoning than they would on Earth. This is due to the lack of gravity causing more blood to flow to the head. This excess blood creates congestion, similar to a cold, which, in turn, diminishes the sense of taste.

## THE SPACE SHUTTLE

Since they were first launched in April 1981, the fleet of space shuttles have flown over 90 missions, ranging from deploying secret military satellites to repairing and servicing the *Hubble Space Telescope* (*see* page 21).

Most recently, the space shuttle *Atlantis* has been undertaking training missions in preparation for the construction of the *International Space Station* (*see* pages 28-29). These missions have included docking with the Russian space station *Mir*.

Here are some interesting facts about the space shuttle –

✳ Largest crew on a space vehicle is on shuttle missions, which can take up to 10 people at once.

✳ The shuttle's cargo bay is 59 ft (18 m) long and 15 ft (4.5 m) wide – big enough to carry a bus.

✳ When the shuttle and *Mir* are docked, they make up the biggest vehicle to orbit the Earth, weighing 200 tons.

*In space, humans have been able to carry out many experiments into the effects of micro-gravity (right). These have included producing crystals and seeing how plants and animals cope without knowing which way is up.*

# International SPACE STATION

Launched in 1986, the *Mir* space station is coming to the end of its career. The next generation of space station will begin with the construction of the *International Space Station (ISS)*. It is a combined effort between the United States, Russia, the European Space Agency, Japan, Canada, and Italy.

Building *ISS* will take about five years, starting in 1997 and it should be completed by about 2003. In total, 44 separate missions will take the individual parts up into orbit. These include flights by American, Russian, and European spacecraft.

When it's finished, the *ISS* will be used for carrying out experiments in space. These will include further studies into the effects of living and working in space (*below*) as well as medical and technological research. A crew of up to six people will live aboard, staying in space for three to five months at a time.

*Showering in space*

The parts of the *ISS* will be built on Earth (*left*) before being taken into space. To start with, ready-built sections (*above*) will be put in orbit and left there. Assembly will begin when the first habitation module is occupied. Once it is finished, the *ISS* will have as much room inside as two large airliners.

## COMPONENTS OF THE ISS

There are two main parts to the *ISS* (*above*) – one Russian and one American. Each of these has living quarters, with its own life-support system. One section has rocket motors that can alter the orbit of the *ISS* around the Earth. There are also European and Japanese laboratories. Power for the *ISS* comes from a huge array of solar panels, which convert sunlight into electricity.

# NEXT CENTURY'S SPACECRAFT

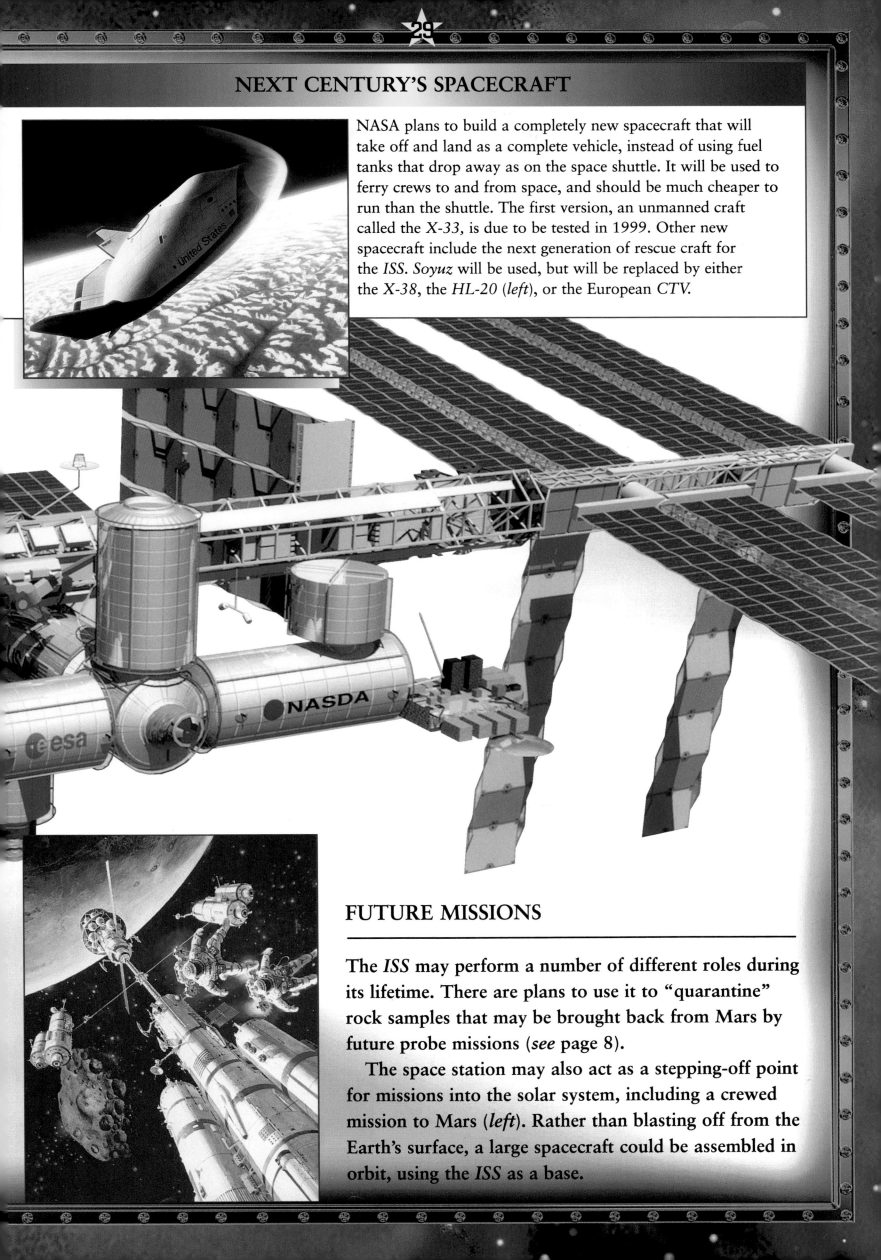

NASA plans to build a completely new spacecraft that will take off and land as a complete vehicle, instead of using fuel tanks that drop away as on the space shuttle. It will be used to ferry crews to and from space, and should be much cheaper to run than the shuttle. The first version, an unmanned craft called the *X-33*, is due to be tested in 1999. Other new spacecraft include the next generation of rescue craft for the *ISS*. *Soyuz* will be used, but will be replaced by either the *X-38*, the *HL-20* (*left*), or the European *CTV*.

## FUTURE MISSIONS

The *ISS* may perform a number of different roles during its lifetime. There are plans to use it to "quarantine" rock samples that may be brought back from Mars by future probe missions (*see* page 8).

The space station may also act as a stepping-off point for missions sinto the solar system, including a crewed mission to Mars (*left*). Rather than blasting off from the Earth's surface, a large spacecraft could be assembled in orbit, using the *ISS* as a base.

# Glossary & TIMELINE

### Antimatter
Matter that is made up of particles that resemble normal particles, but have an opposite electric charge.

### Astronomers
People who study the stars and planets.

### Black holes
The remains of massive stars that have exploded and collapsed in on themselves. The resulting gravity is so strong that not even light can escape from them.

### Charge Coupled Devices
Devices that capture images on a silicon chip rather than photographic film. They are very sensitive and are useful for taking pictures of dim objects.

### Comets
Lumps of ice and dust that orbit around the Sun in a long, looping path.

### Electromagnetic spectrum
The entire range of radiation, ranging from radio waves to gamma rays and including visible light.

### Galaxies
Collections of stars that clump together.

### Gravity
The attractive force of a body. The larger or more dense the body, the greater its gravitational force. A large body, such as the Sun, will have a higher gravitational force than the Earth.

### Light-years
Units used to measure distance in space. One light-year is the distance that a beam of light will travel in a year. This is equivalent to 6 million million miles (10 million million km).

1961 first man in space

1981 launch of first shuttle

1997 launch of ISS

1997 Pathfinder lands on Mars

1977 launch of Voyager probes

1957 launch of Sputnik

1969 first man on Moon

1990 launch of Hubble Space Telescope

## Milky Way
The galaxy that contains our Sun. So-called because it appears as a milky band across the night sky.

## Moons
Small bodies that orbit around some of the major planets.

## Nebulae
Clouds of gas that float about in space. They may be thousands of light-years across. Many nebulae are the remains of stars, thrown off during an explosion, or nova.

## Nova
These occur when one of the stars in a binary system (closely related pair of stars) brightens intensely. Material is pulled from one of the stars onto the other, causing the latter to flare up.

## Orbits
The paths of bodies around another, central body.

## Planets
Bodies that go around a star.

## Probes
Robot devices that explore and examine space.

## Satellites
Objects that orbit a planet. These can be natural, such as moons, or artificial, such as communications satellites.

## Solar System
The group of major planets, including the Earth, and minor planets that orbit the Sun.

## Supernova
An extremely powerful star explosion. The end result may be a black hole.

## Telescopes
Devices that magnify (make bigger) images, allowing us to see very distant objects.

## Universe
The entire system of galaxies, stars, and planets.

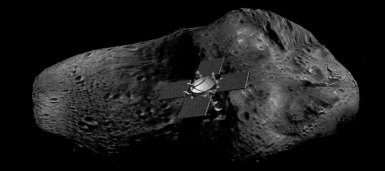

# Index

## PHOTO CREDITS:

*Abbreviations: t-top, m-middle, b-bottom, r-right, l-left*

*All the pictures in this book are by NASA except on the following pages:*

*2, 9b, 19m, 24-25, 28b, 30, 31 & back cover all – Frank Spooner Pictures. 12b, 15m & b, 18 both, 19b, 21 both, 22m, 23, 25m & bl & 27m – Galaxy Picture Library. 22b – Roger Vlitos.*